No, I'm not Drunk!
Taming My Parkinson's With Music, Humor, and Charity

Alan Jackowitz

Copyright © 2014 by Alan Jackowitz
All Rights Reserved

Dedicated to JT – 29 years later, I continue to "put you through hell" and "ruin your sleep." Just making you aware of "being alive." I love you!

Page	Contents
4-5	Preface
6-7	*"No, I'm not Drunk!"*
8-10	Once Upon a Time
11-12	Shake, Rattle and Roll
13-14	Musical Highlights
15-16	Dopamine for $1000 Alex
17	Hurricane Andrew
18-19	Craig Marks
20	Stuart Perlin
21	New York: The Elixir
22-26	NY Stories
27-28	The Story of Arnold
29-30	Early Humor
31-32	Andy
33-34	Charity Wallet
35-37	The Who
38	*"Where's Leo's?"*
39-40	10th Avenue Freeze Out
41-42	True or False?
43-44	Harry Chapin
45	Piano Lessons
46-48	Saturday in the Park with Mike
49-50	"People Who Died"
51-52	"you're gonna have to serve somebody"
53	Today
54-56	V Bar
57-58	*"Why me?"*
58	Acknowledgments
59-61	Judie, Eric, Hayley, Daltrey, Alan

Preface

Whenever I think of memoirs, I think of famous authors with celebrated careers and checkered lives. I do wonder why memoirists are so self-absorbed to think their lives are that inspiring, interesting, or instructional that someone they don't know would drop $15-$25 to read about them. Some writers, though, write for themselves primarily, and the pleasure they get from knowing someone enjoys it, secondarily.

I have a personal story to tell, and I must tell it. It lacks the alcohol of Pete Hammill's, the abuse of *Angela's Ashes* and Mary Karr's, the war record of Eisenhower and Churchill, the courage of John F. Kennedy—or maybe it doesn't. It's the story of a man, a husband, a father, taking a Parkinson's diagnosis in stride—albeit shuffly—and with the help of music, humor, and charity, making a difference in the world. I believe the progression of my disease has slowed due in no small part to my glass-half-full attitude, my looking for silver linings, my tireless efforts in fundraising and awareness, and of course, my medication: Sinemet.

I am celebrating the 7 year anniversary of my Parkinson's disease diagnosis the day before my 50th birthday. While it has stripped me of my brisk walking pace, my dexterity, and my ability to hit a 12 footer (assuming I had it prior), it has enhanced my stamina and given me a new sense of purpose. I see the world in a new way: *Each of us has issues! Everyone!* My new PD glasses allow me to appreciate people in a more sympathetic way. We know the stories of the famous; we don't know the stories of the person next door.

Want to see a hero? Go to Walmart at midnight. The place is populated with African American children and their mama or grandma doing the shopping because they just got off work (the second job) and have no other time to get it done. This nameless woman is a hero.

People have called me *heroic*, and I've laughed or been embarrassed. My life has facets that are far from heroic, but I've lived my PD life with humor, energy, music, attitude, and pills. If *heroic* is too strong, *exemplary* might suffice.

If I can be an example of how to live a life with PD, then I am honored. Perhaps my posting on Facebook sums me up:

> *To the club members of Parkinson's Disease Awareness Group: I certainly appreciate the concerns that anyone would have be it medical, emotional, strategic or otherwise. To ask you to "lighten" it up a little, would be a doing a disservice to the readers who are educated, appeased, or just informed. Allow me to be the (de facto) voice of humor, and calm in this sea of news clips, war stories and unease. Hopefully it'll be as helpful to you, as it is cathartic for me.* (8/29/2014)

To the person who asked, *"How do people actually* die *from Parkinson's?"*—not to belittle your question or your desire for the answer we all want to know—but let's rephrase the question:

Q: How do people actually live with Parkinson's?

A: They continue to do the things they always liked.
They join support groups.
They exercise.
They (try to) make friends with other PDers around the world.
They don't ask, "Why me?"
They laugh when something is funny.
They drool.
They tremble.
They continue to live.

"No, I'm not Drunk!"

I'm walking through the Village on Sunday night, July 2013. It's about midnight, and I'm heading home to my sublet in Battery Park. A light rain is falling; not an extraordinary evening, relatively quiet. As I head west on Bleecker, I hear music seeping out through the door at Paul Colby's legendary club: The Bitter End. Near La Guardia, it has been home to Dylan, Joni, Joan Rivers, Woody Allen, Tom Paxton, Van Morrison, and my son, Eric Jackowitz.

This night, there is a jam session that seems worthy of my attendance. I open the front door and am greeted by a sign in the vestibule announcing a $6 cover. As I reach into my pocket for the money, a large schlub of a man sitting on a stool in the vestibule, seemingly the cover taker/velvet rope tender has an issue with my advancing into the club. He says in a gruff voice that is totally consistent with his Teamster-like appearance, *"You're not going in."*

I can see that the club is not full; my admission denial is based not on the fire marshal's red letter on white oak tag fresco indicating capacity at 194 people. I ask him, *"Why?"* He says, *"You're too drunk—or stoned."*

I'm not much of a drinker, and that night, I hadn't any. The last time I was stoned was before Dylan went electric, so I said, *"No, I'm not."* He insisted I was. I stopped, looked him directly in his large bloodshot eyes, and explained in a forceful tone: *"I am not stoned or drunk or on mushrooms or on any other mind-altering substance. I have Parkinson's disease. The uninformed misread my masked expression as that of drunkenness. Please, let me in. Besides, if I'm going to look drunk or stoned, I want to be drunk or stoned."*

He let me in.

The very next week, I read that he died. He fell down the stairs at the club.
I guess you could say that he came to his bitter end.

Once Upon a Time

March 2007

I started a new job as Controller of a full service insurance agency. There were about 50 employees, doing about 10 million dollars of business. Soon after starting work, one man, came up to me and said, you really must have had a rough arm injury as it doesn't swing when you walk. I had no idea. What was evident to me was a small tingle that travelled down my left arm to my third fingertip. I made an appointment to see Dr. Ruskin-neurologist, he didn't say anything upon meeting me, only to send me for a "Brain scan" I did an internal invisible double take and said to myself B-r-a-i-n S-c-a-n?????
I subsequently learned that the MRI was to rule out things, like stroke or tumor. He knew immediately upon seeing me--Parkinson's Disease.
His partner was very reassuring by saying it isn't terminal and that no 2 cases were alike, and no one progresses at a predetermined fast or slow pace. He didn't even prescribe medicine at that time. He recommended that I get a second opinion from Dr. Carlos Singer at the University of Miami. My wife was with me during the results meeting with Ruskin's partner, she was incredibly supportive. I'm scheduled to have lunch with my father the next day.

Everyone has seen The Godfather. There is a famous scene-I think they are all famous where there is to be a meeting in the Bronx at an Italian restaurant where Clemenza's men know where they can hide a gun. The meeting was between the "Turk" Solozzo, Capt McCluskey, and Michael Corleone. They sit down, begin to talk in Sicilian while McCluskey stuffs his napkin in his shirt collar as a bib and begins to eat. Michael asks permission to get up and use the bathroom. Mccluskey frisks him as he leaves the table and then the pressure mounts.   The sound of the subway screech and the

Carmine Coppola conducted orchestra only serves to increase the tension. Michael fiddles with the back of the toilet tank and finds the gun duct taped to the back of the high-up toilet tank. He finishes peeing, washes his hands and proceeds to walk back to the table. He sits down at the table and for 5 seconds pretends to listen to Solozzo continue to talk in Sicilian. He gets up and fires a shot in Mccluskey's forehead , another in Solozzo's.   Mccluskey continues to chew for about 2-3 seconds and then his head falls face down on the table. My father, also with a delayed reaction, was Mccluskey.   Difference being Arthur Avenue in the Bronx became University Drive in Sunrise, Florida. Louis' became Pastrami King, and oh yeah this was real life.

I thought that I had found a home for good. Interesting characters, the agency was run by 2 very high strung brothers who screamed at the top of their lungs at the drop of any hat. They hated each other's guts, fired more people in my first year there then I saw fired in my previous 27 years of working combined. They often rehired them and refired them . The next level down was the Producers-Salespeople who made a fortune of money and were still treated like chattel by their employers. This place was a hotbed of angst, back stabbing, disrespect, and a ton of revenue. It is now incomprehensible to me that the amount of money earned by the large insurance companies is so high as to pay fortunes in commission and advertising and naming rights and bonus checks, and corporate greed, and still make a substantial profit. I illustrate it here only to demonstrate the level of distrust and paranoia that the employees -including me - lived with each day. This only adds to the stressful day- a known trigger of the disease.

One example of such mistrust was what had to have been the bugging of my office. A general memo was sent out to the employees that said to curtail the listening of music through the broadband connection at the office. Understandable. Also understandable would be the monitoring of the usage if someone was not following the new rules. What was not understandable was the immediate confrontation in my office after I put on a CD. Telling me to shut off the music, I attempted to explain that the CD was not affecting the broadband connection.   He said, "I don't care, turn off the music." I realized that the only way he could have known was through a bug as his office was clear across the building. This was confirmed to me by the person who placed the bug.

Early on, my symptoms were unrecognizable to the layman.   It made it easy to keep it secret. More importantly, the fuhrer who was my boss wouldn't fire me if he didn't know, although his review of the medicine list might have given me away. He would take his employee list, mark it with the anecdotally generated list of employee illnesses and keep a mental tab of their real and potential costs to the business.

Both examples, clearly illegal, are just to demonstrate the stress of the job and the gradual progression of the disease; perhaps at a more rapid pace because of it.

Shake Rattle and Roll

When I was a kid and began to do crossword puzzles with my mother at a much too early age, I remember that many puzzles had the clue Impresario Hurok. Of course the answer is Sol. Spanish word for sun would be too easy, you'd think there would be a middle difficulty for the word. Maybe the needle pulling thread. I remember asking about the term impresario. I think that when it comes down to it, it's a fancy term for concert promoter.
 Impresarios then, by extension, would now include Bill Graham, John Scher, Ron Delsener, George Wein, and Alan Jackowitz and Rick Harris.

I've always wanted to promote concerts. I think it goes no deeper than wanting the ability to show my all-access pass to the security team. I don't need only blue M&Ms.

 It was Early December 2011 when I decided to promote a charity event with all proceeds going to the National Parkinson Foundation. I quickly enlisted the help of my friend, Dr. Rick Harris, he also of gray hair, love of music and impulsive tendencies. Let's get this going before we think what the hell are we doing. When would be the worst time to hold a concert, especially when we wanted to enlist corporate sponsorships—Christmas of course. Those corporations who would otherwise be amenable to making such a donation would be hard pressed to do it right before the holidays.
   Press on-more important considerations. If I'm going to be the promoter, then I want to put my imprint on it. My son, Eric went through high school, playing in a few bands with his friends. He is an extraordinary drummer. It seemed that I was a roadie, carrying his drum gear from gig to gig. One of the most popular spots was Murphy's Law. This was a bar, and yes the band members were way too young to shave, let along drink alcohol.

Something about the whole scene struck me as one big positive. The afternoon was billed as a battle of the bands. A dozen or so bands were assigned times to show up and play their half hour set. The winner of the afternoon was adjudged so, right before the announcement at around 6pm The criteria was not crowd decibel level, or local newspaper critic opinion, or applause o meter. It was very methodical, with no room for misinformation. The winner of the competition was the band that brought the most people with them to watch and to pay the 10 dollar cover. Perfect! Everybody wins! The young band gets a chance to play before their friends and perhaps some of the people who played just before or after them. The bar makes out because it is always on a dead afternoon where business would suffer anyway. Parents and grandparents get to kvell.

We decided to emulate this scenario, except the beneficiary of the afternoon would be the National Parkinson Foundation, instead of the bar. More people win. Deciding on a beneficiary was rather simple. Through my friend Ken Hartmann, I got a chance to meet the CEO of the NPF. We met for coffee in Coral Gables, late one Friday afternoon. After exchanging pleasantries, and a little small talk, she proceeded with "How can we help you?" My response, allowing us to help you help us.

Musical Highlights

Everyone has Songs that evoke a smile or a tear from a day gone by. Here are some of mine:

"Pure and Easy" – The Who
Played when Judie and I first got together. I was playing DJ, instead of her.

"Our Love is Here to Stay" – George and Ira Gershwin
We got married to this song.

"Smokin' in the Boys' Room" – Brownsville Station
Played at the wedding; an ill-conceived idea.

"Up for the Down Stroke" – George Clinton
Favorite song from the concert following George's degree ceremony.
Eric played drums.

"In the Summertime" – Mungo Jerry
1970 car ride to Florida; every time we turned on the radio, it was on.

"Pachalafaka" – performed by Soupy Sales
Wrote a skit about the song in camp.
Then learned it was written by my Great Uncle.

"Too Darn Hot" – from *Kiss Me, Kate*
Eric and Hayley loved it on the way to school.
Became a launching pad for both in school plays.

"Build Me Up Buttercup" – The Foundations

      My sister, Lori – age 2, dancing to it on "Wonderama" on channel 5.

"Suite: Judy Blue Eyes" – Crosby, Stills, & Nash
      Song played by Spitz at Canteen.

"Sunday" – *Sunday in the Park with George*
      Hayley killed it at competition.

Dopamine for $1000 Alex

I was on Jeopardy. Right, I was the guy who was shaking his head and his buzzer hand, and probably mouthing 4 letter words, when in my eagerness to say, *"Who is Rocky Colavito?"* I buzzed in too soon. This let the schoolteacher from Shaker Heights slide right in and answer the question—question the answer—correctly. This was in the beginning of the second season of Jeopardy under Alex Trebek's reign. During the Art Fleming years, you were allowed to buzz in as soon as the clue was revealed. This allowed those fast readers or category experts to at least have first chance at the clue.

I flew out on my dime, stayed with friends, and my friend Steve Synott even came to the taping. When we got to the studio, I immediately recognized a few things: the typical Jeopardy contestant *is* boring and conservative. Thanks to the '50s quiz show scandal, the staff kept an eye on us at all times. Neither a vending machine snack, nor a quick pee went unsupervised.

They film a week's worth of shows in one day, which makes for a very long day—like a class trip complete with overzealous chaperones, bag lunches, and the buddy system. Contestants were hardly allowed to talk, so I stayed entertained by mulling over the threat my brother made as I was leaving for LA: *"If you get an Audio Daily Double right, I'll blow you!"* (I think it would have been illegal even without the incest angle.) Luckily, I didn't even land on one.

I did get some right: al dente, Harvey Milk, Newfoundland. I mean, *"What is al dente, Harvey Milk, and Newfoundland?"* Going into Final Jeopardy, I had a reasonable chance to win. The Final Jeopardy answer was *"Which of Columbus's 3 ships never made it back to Spain?"*
Santa Maria. That's etched in my brain.

Trivia has always been an important part of my life. Didn't everyone read the Encyclopedia Britannica while listening to Mott the Hoople after school? When the '80s came around, I was a prize pick for trivial pursuit teams.

If only I could dump some of the minutiae from my brain. I don't need to remember who played Glinda the Good Witch in *The Wizard of Oz*. I don't even have to remember that her name was Glinda. Or that Nolan Ryan is from Alvin, Texas. Or that Hubert Humphrey's middle name was Horatio. Or that the "S" in Harry S. Truman doesn't stand for anything.

Let's do a systemwide purge of my brain and free up some valuable cranial real estate for some new dopamine manufacturing plants. I'll gladly trade in my knowledge of Thurman Munson's career stats for a shuffleless gait.

Hurricane Andrew

Naïveté can be a good thing; ignorance is often bliss.

Sometime in the middle of the night on August 24, 1992, I got a phone call from our neighbor. Hurricane Andrew was cutting through the Florida peninsula like a buzz saw. Luckily, we still had phone service, even though our cable and electricity were both out. Our neighbor, a woman alone, called and asked me if I could hear or feel the roof of our attached townhouse peel off. I told her, *"Nawwwwww, roofs don't fall off here; that only happens to poor Caribbean island houses with shoddy construction, probably just damage from some flying debris."*

I put her at ease, not because of my soothing voice and demeanor, but because of my naïveté. I thought it was the truth, but when I opened the front door at 8:00am, the first things that came to mind were *Dresden* and *Hiroshima*. The next thing was *"Why are there munchkins singing on what was our lawn? Are the Keebler elves on strike? Are the munchkins scabs?"* I realized that our common roof was in pieces on the ground, and people were gathering.

When I established that we were all okay, I began to help our neighbors and the community. The cleanup took weeks, and my contribution was directing traffic at the junction of Florida's Turnpike and Kendall Drive. The army flew down to help with rebuilding. I felt like a firefighter calendar pinup when a female soldier handed me a burger and commented on my nice legs. Who says charity is all altruism?

The next weekend, I drove down to Homestead and helped to distribute meals to displaced families. It was during this two-week period that I realized what I like in the world of charitable endeavors. I found I'd much rather be in the trenches than in the boardroom. Getting my hands dirty makes me feel more helpful.

Craig Marks

The value of exercise as part of the treatment is arguably the biggest development in the caring of PD patients. When I was first diagnosed in 2007, I had a laundry list of concerns and questions for Dr. Singer. Chief among them was about how exercise might help to slow the disease's progression. Back in 2007, the answer was *"It won't."* In 2014, the answer is *"It most definitely will."* So as not to cast aspersions on Dr. Singer, it is worth noting that he did recommend exercise as part of a daily routine, but to help keep limber, not to slow the disease. This is what all the doctors thought at the time.

Approximately two years later, my mother saw a news spot about a doctor in Ohio who was treating PD patients with a boxing regimen, yielding great results. My bag was packed. But before I ventured to Ohio, I searched Florida for a similar program and found one nearby.

Craig Marks is a physical therapist. Trained at the University of Tennessee, he now works in Cooper City, and his 5'6" frame casts a much longer shadow. His father died of complications from PD, so Craig decided to give to the community what he began for his Dad: a physical therapy routine developed specifically for the PD patient. The issues of balance, shuffling gait, and rigidity are all addressed in his sessions. With Craig, you get more than just the nuts and bolts of physical exercise—your local gym provides that. You also get an ear, a supportive training partner, and in many cases like mine, a friend. Even though he says I hit him like a sledgehammer.

But that's not all. Fellini could hardly do better in providing a cast of characters more eccentric. Over the years, I've seen Craig Moody morph into an exercise machine and one of Broward County's eligible bachelors. I've met Arlette, who would rather be anywhere else, and whose disdain is so palpable that the group circuit training almost blows a fuse. Silvia saves the day. Her energy, hard work, and audible Monica Seles's grunts keep the class on track.

The man among boys is Bob Schwartz. A cross between the muscles of The Rock, the charm of Paul Newman, and the physical appearance of Wallace Shawn, he is my partner in PD training. At 72 years old, he commands respect for his diligence and his knowledge of 70-year-old music. Though it's difficult to exercise with a Rudy Vallee megaphone in tow, it was his slow, deliberate, decent onto a gym bench that begat the gym's unofficial motto: *"Don't Sit On Your Scrotum!"*

The National Parkinson Foundation has awarded Craig a grant so that he can provide free or reduced cost training to the PD community. Nobody could be more deserving!

Stuart Perlin

Every cause needs a leader, a lightning rod, a larger than life loud New Yorker—the one that stirs the drink. Upon the (eventual) retirement of the current NPF CEO, a conclave of the college of NPF Board of Directors should be held. When the puff of white smoke appears, Stuart Perlin should get the big hat. Stuart is a gruff, pussycat of a man who is President of the South Palm Beach chapter of NPF. My nickname for him is Mr. Wolf because, like the guy in *Pulp Fiction*, Stuart is the problem solver.

I met Stuart at a support group meeting in Boca and instantly realized that we spoke the same language. Every Saturday morning, he co-hosts a radio show devoted to (1) professionals discussing their latest projects and studies and (2) the average guy. I was asked to be interviewed, and it didn't take me long to say, *"Yes!"*

Two questions still stick with me some 3 months after the show.
"Is there anything good about Parkinson's?"
"If you ever get down, what do you do to help you get back up?"

Good things about Parkinson's:
- not a thing

Pick-me-ups?
- The Clash

Stuart's dedication to the PD community is steadfast.
Thank you, Stuart.

New York: The Elixir

As you approach NYC from the air, it starts in Philadelphia. By train, it begins at Metropark. By car, it's Newark airport. By boat, Perth Amboy, NJ. I'm referring, of course, to the palpable adrenaline rush that surges as NYC comes into view and beckons to you. The brain responds in its own language, complete with axons, dendrites, and synapses, but it all translates to dopamine. Dopamine. *Dopamine*.

The story of NY has been told countless times, but NY as medicine? Not too often. The tinkling of the piano playing the first notes of NY, NY. The party line says Liza Minnelli's version is trite, played out. The party line says Frank's is the anthem. Liza's is the inspiration. *My neck loosens up.*

Go down into the subway at West 4th. Pass the guy preparing to take a dump on the platform, hurry! Look across to the uptown trains. Note the trio playing "Take the A Train." Maybe they're students from NYU. Or the New School. Or maybe it's the reincarnation of the Duke himself. They're good. My train arrives. I shuffle to the platform edge and breathe a sigh of relief that I got in without trouble. I get out at Prospect Park—suburbia celebrate Brooklyn! Robert Plant is delivering the Zeppelin songbook with other musicians. Page is great, but Billy No Name will suffice. The guitar riff can only mean one thing: "Whole Lotta Love." I ain't foolin. *I'm walking with a purpose.*

Go to Vbar! Matt's holding court with Paul and Ricky and Nate and Krystle and Francesca. Playing Ray Charles, Little Feat, Big Maybelle, and then, at a quarter to three—not 2:45—we hear Frank, "So set 'em up Joe." *I'm dancing!!*

NY Stories

I call it a swagger. My gait? Faster, steadier. My posture? Taller, prouder. Why? NY, NY. It's simple: when I'm there, my health improves. Is it in my head? I almost don't care what the answer is, but Dr. Gilbert at NYU's neurology clinic says, "No. It most definitely can be real." Her analogy is that of the tandem bike. The Parkinsonian passenger on the tandem bike achieves greater therapeutic value than the driver. It's what's called forced exercise. In my case, walking the streets of NY is my forced exercise.

During the summer of 2011, I decided I needed to do what I could to spend more time there. I packed a bag, got on a plane, and thought of a way to solve what I thought was lacking in NYC: walking tours for the elderly and physically challenged. I created a company called Slow Afoot. I stayed with friends and in cheap hotels, whatever I had to do to make it work and keep myself in NYC.

As it turned out, the only thing slow about the business was its ability to get people to take a tour. I quickly stopped giving tours, but I still think it's a good idea and hope to resurrect it.

Joan Evatt, from Australia, was one of my tour takers, and she wrote these beautiful blog entries about me. I promise, I didn't have them commissioned.

NEW YORK STORIES part 1—where anything and everything is possible.
Posted on August 9, 2011 by boeufblogginon

Ground Zero

I met a man.

Well, you know how it is. It's your first morning in New York after a 24+hour plane flight. You wake up at 3:30am and are unable to get back to sleep. So 5am sees you exploring the hotel, and getting acquainted with the night staff who are rapidly approaching the end of their shift.

I end up in the IT section with a bank of computers that I cannot get started. My intention is to send quick messages to my nearest and dearest at home to say His Nibs and I have arrived safe 'n sound.

There is a man who, with hotel staff in attendance, is also not sleeping. He offers me the use of his Ipad to send my quick messages home. I accept and we fall into a conversation.

His name is Alan Jackowitz. He's about my age, probably a few years younger. A New Yorker by birth, he is articulate, witty and intelligent with that wonderful NY view of the world he inhabits. He also suffers from Parkinson's Disease.

We talk for a couple of hours during which the sun rose, the cock crows and the hotel staff change shifts. A member of staff periodically comes by to check that he is OK.

From politics to the law, the role of the media, entertainment and sport – no subject went untouched, no opinion not given. He is a doer. Earlier in the year he organised a charity concert for Parkinson's research in Florida where he now lives. The concert was called SHAKE, RATTLE AND ROLL which made me hoot with laughter. He is a very funny man.
Alan gossiping over a beer.

For the last 15 years or more he has been living in Florida. A tingle in one finger was the forerunner to a diagnosis that has profoundly changed his life.

Alan came to NY for a 2 week visit in February this year and now cannot go back home. For some reason the over stimulating environment of New York – the bustle, sounds, the pace and the physical challenges of living in New York are beneficial to Parkinson sufferers. Within a week of his visit the symptoms had started to diminish.

The problem for Alan, a former accountant, was how to return to New York, and find a job so that he could move his family back here. This has proved no easy task. New York, like so much of the US, is still feeling the brunt of the global financial crisis. Employment is difficult for all – if you're older and disabled it is bloody nigh impossible!

Alan's answer to this problem is to start a business. He is in the process of setting up as a travel guide to the aged, the infirm and the disabled – a niche market he understands totally.

He asks me whether His Nibs and I would be interested in being guinea pigs for his first trial walking tour of the World Trade Centre and Wall Street financial district. We were keen as were our two close friends with whom we were travelling.

So two days later we all met Alan and his daughter, Hayley, at the appointed time and place. The next one and a half to two hours are spent slowly meandering around the WTC site and NY's financial district. We end up in a pub in a museum having a beer and giving Alan a SWOT analysis of the tour.

The great thing about local guides is the passion for their home town. A mixture of historical fact, personal input and old fashioned gossip is an essential requirement for a guide to give a successful two hour live stand-up. They personalise the bricks and mortar, making what you see come alive. Alan lost loved ones on 9/11. Unlike many who are still unable, he can talk about it.

A quiet moment of contemplation for His Nibs overlooking Ground

Zero.

I have always been uneasy about visiting ground zero when in NY, but the one thing I've noticed since my last visit to New York two years ago, is the growing pride New Yorkers are expressing at the reconstruction of the WTC site. Everyone asks you have you been to ground zero yet and, if so, what do you think of it. They want to know. It is a little weird as if the city needs constant approval by outsiders of what is being done. They shouldn't need reassurance but are constantly seeking it. Construction is going ahead at break neck speed. Crews work 24/7 at the site, buildings are being erected at a floor per week. The whole site is taking shape.

It is almost ten years and New Yorkers seem to be coming to the realisation that until the site is finished it remains a weeping wound. The care taken with the design of ground zero is evident. The innovative visitors' centre and the memorial are gobsmackingly beautiful. The city will be better when there is no longer a hoarding, a cement truck, a construction worker or a crane to be seen in the area. And so New Yorkers continue to confront and overcome a most traumatic part of their history which they are doing with passion, gritty determination, great gusto and reverence tinged with both sadness and humour.

And so to Alan Jackowitz. Alan's enthusiasm and optimism in setting up this new venture is infectious. Professional obstacles, and there are many, can be overcome because he's already overcome so many personal ones. What he is facing at a personal level the city has been facing for ten years as a community.

Alan, as the city has done, goes forth to face what can only be described as the most daunting task with great courage and humour, well aware of what must be done if his business is to succeed.

New York is one of my three favourite cities in the world. It is constantly re-inventing itself, one of the reasons why it continues to appeal and stay relevant; it never settles for a moment, and there is an unfailing optimism, a genuine fundamental belief that anything and everything is possible. Alan Jackowitz is the personification of that belief.

The Story of Arnold

Slow Afoot Walking Tours is in high gear not giving walking tours. As the proprietor, I had a small, finite money supply, and more was going out than coming in. I had two weeks left to make this business work, and I had to conserve as much as possible.

My M.O. was Priceline hotels with a limit of $100 per night. The demand for hotel rooms in NYC is amazingly volatile. The technology that allows a room to be sold at a discount via Priceline also allows the Holiday Inn Wall Street to be sold for $100 one night and $400 the very next day. The auto show can wipe out the hotel room supply in one fell swoop.

This week was one of those weeks. I went to Newark airport to get a cheap hotel, and while it certainly saved me money, it also cost me bodily wear and tear.

I booked a room at the Affinia on 1st and 44th, and checked my bags with the bell captain. When I arrived later than evening to retrieve them, I waited with one of the bell staff: let's call him Arnold. We'll call him Arnold because his parents named him Arnold some 50 years earlier. After chatting with him about New York Mets history, including Cleon Jones, Ron Swoboda, and Ed Kranepool, it seemed like we knew each other well.

I stepped away to get my bags, and when I returned to say *"goodbye"* to Arnold, he told me he had given a cabbie a $20 dollar bill to take me wherever I wanted to go. He also said not to bother arguing with him because he had already paid and couldn't get a refund. I thanked him vociferously and went on my way.

August 2012:

I'm in a car with the Waldmans, and we pass the Affinia. I ask them to stop the car, so I can ask about Arnold. The staff said he no longer works there, but they think he works at the Intercontinental on 9th avenue. We were going in that direction anyway, so we stopped, so I could again ask about Arnold. He was there! I asked if he remembered me. He said of course he did. I pulled out a $20 dollar bill to reimburse him. He refused the money, dismissing it out of hand, and told me to pay it forward. I am doing just that, often thinking of his willingness to give with no mind to what he might get back.

Early Humor

I don't know where it started, but I've been laughing and trying to make other people laugh for as long as I can remember. Perhaps it was the pediatrician's office, with "Goofus and Gallant" in *Highlights* magazine, or "Laughter is the Best Medicine" in *Reader's Digest*. It was probably my father, and his ability to command a room by telling jokes. He'd sell you a joke. He was the guy who could sell the proverbial ice cube to an Eskimo, and you'd start laughing way before the punch line ever arrived.

As a little kid, I watched Ed Sullivan on Sunday nights as he exposed a few standup comedians each week: George Carlin and his hippy dippy weatherman, Richard Pryor, Jack E. Leonard, Charlie Callas, Buddy Hackett, George Gobel, Jackie Vernon. This exposure, plus the last 5 minutes of Carson each night, provided my exposure to stand up comedy. It wasn't until Comedy Central came along that the standup comedian became so prevalent in popular culture.

As a child of the '60s, TV was quite important to me. All 6 channels. We devoured shows like *Hogan's Heroes*, *My Mother the Car*, *Green Acres*, *Petticoat Junction*, *Julia*, and *Get Smart*.
A sampling of the situations from which the comedy was extracted:
- A woman reincarnated as a 1928 Porter automobile.
- The zany and madcap hijinks of a WWII prison camp.
- A CIA agent with a shoe phone.

The Catskill Mountains in Southeast NY are approximately 2 hours from NYC. It was a weekend getaway destination for NY Jews who wanted to escape the city and eat until they exploded. Jews have an affinity for overeating, and Catskill resorts like the Concord, Raleigh, Homowack, Kutsher's, and Tamarack did nothing to change the stereotype. You'd get there for dinner on Friday night, and eat incessantly until Sunday lunch. The ride back home certainly included farting, belching, belt buckle loosening, and general feelings of uncomfortability. But a good Alka-Seltzer or Pepto-Bismol could make you forget about it quickly.

The raunchy resort shows would make us laugh so hard that we didn't notice the cigarette stench, vomit stains, and general physical disrepair. What we remembered was Morty Gunty, Larry Alpert, John Raitt, and Allan Jones, despite their being the parents of some more famous stars such as Jack Jones and Bonnie Raitt.

There were 2 shows each night, with the late show being a little bluer. You knew you had made it when you were allowed to stay up for the late show. It was during these shows that commanding respect crossed paths with dirty, funny jokes that stay with me today. And while I don't have the stage presence of a Seinfeld, Lewis Black, or Arthur Jackowitz, I do pretty well.

Andy

I met Andy Neiman in September of 1979. I know the date well because my first job out of school was as if it was the first semester of graduate school. In 1979, it was called "the big 8." No, not the collegiate athletic conference: the 8 largest, worldwide accounting firms. They settled on 8 because there was a big drop-off between numbers 8 and 9. Today, through merger and scandal, it's down to 3.

There is a lot of truth to the stereotypical reputation of accountants: conservative and far from the life of the party. That green eyeshade is not far off, but put them in a setting of a 2 week training school, where alcohol is available, and watch out! It's still a far cry from a music conference, but many accounting pronouncements were formulated during moments of inebriation at accounting conferences. Who can forget FASB 8 on capital leases?

Andy and I immediately became friends at our school in Atlantic City, our basic training before we were to ship out to our new post in Washington, D.C. We are both New York area Jews, our families steeped in mom and pop style small business. Working for Coopers & Lybrand was a far cry from that. I believe that the culture clash provided as much of the disenchantment as the work. We were both gone from that world within three years. However, We certainly managed to sneak in some fun. We would find happy hours and eat the free appetizers for dinner. I think our weekly attendance at the Greenery's "all we could eat" mussels helped put them out of business. Kobayashi could not have done better! One night when we sat at the end of the bar, the bartender put down a burger waiting to be picked up for delivery to a table. We ate it. I'm not saying we were crazy, but in the accounting world, we were

Richard Pryor and Robin Williams.

We made a pact. We vowed that if one of us died prematurely, the survivor would tell a joke at the funeral. Luckily, that has not been necessary. However, when I told Andy of my diagnosis, I was sure to mention that jokes are not off-limits. He proceeded to tell me the one where the elderly woman maintains a relationship with a particular elderly man because she doesn't have to buy batteries anymore—he has Parkinson's disease.

Charity Wallet

I was born and raised down in Alabama, on a farm way back up . . . wait. That's not me. Those are the opening lines to "Patches" by Clarence Carter. I was born and raised in Brooklyn in 1957. Perhaps it's the sepia toned glow of nostalgia of those days that remains in my mind's eye that makes it resonate today. Maybe the simpler times were better. Or maybe ages 1-12 are precious wherever you grow up because of the formative nature of those years. At that time, the only problem I faced was which color of "Billy the Kid" Dungarees with the reinforced knee I should wear. Playing punchball in the PS 115 schoolyard took care of the knees, even If it was reinforced 12 times.

Living in a row house in Brooklyn in the 1960s was idyllic! It could have been Tara. The Canarsie section of Brooklyn was named for the mighty Canarsie Indians. If you did a genealogical study of the area, you would find that the population mix, when traced all the way back to the time of the Indians, would show that the tribal chief was probably an Italian Jew. For a long time, I thought those were the only two types of people in the world. I guess the cohabitation works well because of the similarities of the two types of people, starting with the family and food, and extending all the way down to the prevalence of feminine facial hair.

It was there that my first encounter with charity came to light. I was walking on East 86th when I came upon a man's wallet lying open on the street. The license revealed the rightful owner, and I went to return it. When I walked up the flight of steps to the front door of the house, the old woman who lived there greeted me. I told her I found the wallet on the street with a few dollars intact. She was overwhelmed by my honesty. She said that she needed to give me a reward but didn't have one to give me. She asked me very sweetly if I was Jewish. When I answered "yes," she said, *"Well then, can I give you a kiss?"*

As I put this story on paper, I realize it may be a story of prejudice as well as charity. Would she not have kissed me if I wasn't Jewish? Who knows; the passing of time can play tricks in your mind.

The Who

June 14, 1974. Robert's birthday. Sitting fourth row to the right at Madison Square
Garden for the last night of The Who's five night residency. I think my other Who fan friends—Randy Prus, Tim Brasko, Alan Kabus, and Joe Razzano—saw them earlier in the week. Robert, Lisa Spiegel, and I all paid the ransom like sum of $20 to a ticket broker for the privilege of temporary deafness. If The Who didn't do it, then Ronnie Montrose did with his half hour set of feedback. I think the clinical definition of temporary deafness is a ringing in the speaker screaming ear for up to, and including, forty years. It will either go away or be called permanent. It doesn't really matter. The excitement from that night still resonates. *Quadrophenia* remains my favorite album.

Why is the concert ending, instrument destruction portion of the evening's program included in The Who's concert evaluation? In typical teenage one-upmanship, we reported to each other: *"On Monday, we saw them destroy three guitars!" "Oh yeah? On Friday, we saw Keith Moon insert a bass drum in his bum!!"* It's funny how exaggeration grows over time. He would have done the crash cymbal, but the high hats were already there.

My love affair with The Who began with the release of *Live at Leeds*. Their cover of Mose Allison's "Young Man Blues" could *or should* be the anthem for all teenage rebellion. They took Eddie

Cochrane's "Summertime Blues" and changed it from a pop ditty to a rocker. "Magic Bus" went on too long. But the Tommy interlude was magical.

1971 brought us *Who's Next*. From Christgau to Bangs, pound for pound, the critics' favorite Who album. This album validates the need for the compact disc or digital configuration. I played side one of the album without venturing onto the other side where "Baba O'Riley" and "The Song is Over" lie in dormancy waiting for my album flip. I was too busy with "Getting in Tune," "Substitute," "Behind Blue Eyes," and "Won't Get Fooled Again" to be bothered by what is truly classic rock, and too lazy to get up and flip the album.

We moved to New Jersey in 1970. East Brunswick was a favorite destination for the white flight from NYC. WNEW had a contest called COMMENT, where listeners would speak their mind and receive an album. My keen observation of more trees in suburbia, than urbia, earned me *Christmas and the Beads of Sweat* by Laura Nyro. All this proactivism stood me in good stead as my deluge of post cards for another event earned me two tickets to the world premier of *Tommy* the movie.

The baseball writers have it right when they say that a player must wait five years before being placed on the ballot for election to the hall of fame. You need the retrospective viewpoint to judge a career. That night at the Ziegfeld, we saw the best movie ever. My opinion was buttressed by our meeting of Angela Lansbury, Pete Townshend, Keith Moon, Tony Perkins, and famous DJ and pedophile, Dave Herman. With the advent of movie rentals years later, Ann-Margret in baked beans was less sensual, and not at all entertaining compared to what we saw at the premiere. It was the worst movie ever.

Even in their tragedy, there are lessons to be learned. In light of Cincinnati, don't rush the stage. In light of Keith Moon, moderation please. In light of John Entwistle, act your age. He was arguably rock's best bassist, yet provides the model for interchangeability. In every rock 'n roll magazine in every year through the '70s, John Entwistle was voted best bass player. As a fifty something-year-old man, the night before their tour was to start in Las Vegas, he dropped dead of a heart attack after a night of cocaine. For all you musicians out there, unless you are the song writer or the front man, you are replaceable. This founding member of The Who was replaced by by Pino Palladino in 24 hours.

I've seen them numerous times since then, and the last time was the best. They did Quadrophenia. I stood and danced the entire time, impressing those around me. But all I was doing was self medicating. My PD was gone that night.

Oh, by the way, I remember they came back for an encore. I swear it was because we didn't stop applauding.

"Where's Leo's?"

It's a summer Sunday morning—about 8am. Hayley and I are riding Citi Bikes through town. We are down near Wall Street, and I am looking for a bagel place called Leo's. I'd been to Leo's before—great bagels.

The financial district is noted for its cobblestones, history, and streets that are impossible to negotiate. We continue to ride, getting hungrier.

We happen upon a large young man in a red jumpsuit with the following emblazoned on it: *Wall Street Development*. In an act of anti-stereotypical masculinity, I approach the man and ask, *"Do you know how to get to Leo's Bagels?"* He thinks for a second, looks me in the eye, and says, *"Yes!"*

I like this guy immediately because of his sarcasm and playfulness. I reply, *"Would you kindly impart this information to me before I expire?"*

He quickly gives me the directions, and I ask him, *"What would you like to eat?"* He answers a bagel with cream cheese and a Dr. Brown's Black Cherry. I say, *"thanks,"* and get moving to Leo's.

After Hayley and I eat breakfast, I fill Red's order, and we go looking for him. When I find him and he sees me carrying his parcel, he says, *"Holy shit! Can't believe you actually bought it!"* He reaches out and gives me a fist pound.

I lean close to him and say, *"I never fuck around when it comes to bagels."*

10ᵗʰ Avenue Freeze Out

Sounds like the Jeopardy answer to "What do you call a Parkinson's episode on the west side of Manhattan?"

The Boss! Given his playing pool/skipping school/acting real cool background, I'm sure that few would have predicted such a high degree of sophistication that his lyrics have morphed into, or the sheer magnitude of community giveback his career has allowed him to champion.

I don't think he knows this, but he and I go back a long way together. When he was singing about cars and girls in Freehold, NJ, in 1970, I was singing my bar mitzvah 15 miles up Route 9 in East Brunswick. Whenever I'm asked where I am from. I always say NY, except if we're talking about Bruce. Then, it's Exit 9!

In the summer of '75, Bruce was on the covers of both *Time* and *Newsweek*. The summer of Bruce culminated with a series of concerts at the Bottom Line in New York City. I was away for the summer, therefore knew none of this.

I began as a freshman at Georgetown that September, and rumors were rampant that Bruce was to play a concert at the Georgetown gym. Georgetown was full of Jersey people, so this was huge, but no one knew when tickets were going on sale. I was walking by the box office when up went the window, and presto! I had tickets and new friends in a DC minute.

I sat second row center and have been a great fan ever since. Other Bruce concert stories include the time when I pleaded with the ticket manager to let me in after the show started and after the box office was closed. After a 5 second pause for contemplation, he asked me to name 5 Bruce songs—the concert was great.

My love affair with Bruce was solidified upon hearing the story of his involvement with the 9/11 survivors. I always knew he was a very generous, charitable man, but this was special. Many of the people who died were NJ residents. The *New York Times* published obituaries for everyone who died, and many mentioned love affairs with Bruce's music. Bruce contacted every survivor.

His concerts are legendary; his sense of humanity and charity is saintly.

True or False?

"Light of Day" is

- a movie starring Joan Jett and Michael J. Fox
- a Bruce Springsteen song
- the name of a Jersey Shore music festival raising money and awareness for the treatment and cure of Parkinson's disease
- all of the above

While I was living in NY, I heard about the work done by Bob Benjamin and the Light of Day Foundation. They run a series of approximately 50 concerts held around the world. When I learned about the extent of their influence, I decided I had to meet them. It was April or May of 2011, and they were producing a concert at the Count Basie Theatre in Red Bank, NJ. The concert featured Alejandro Escovedo and Jesse Malin.

I got to Red Bank via a NJ transit train at about show time. I didn't know a soul and didn't know for sure if Bob was going to be there, or even what he looked like. What I did know is that everybody I met was totally egoless, very helpful, and completely accommodating. After his set, I went to the merch table and met Jesse Malin. The merch table had t-shirts, buttons, and other artist accessories for sale. Unless you are Jay-Z, Beyoncé, or Iggy Azalea, the merch table provides the total amount of $ that today's musician can make. Jesse introduced me to Tony Pallagrosi, and between the two of them, they made sure I had a chance to meet the founder of the Light of Day Foundation, Bob Benjamin.

Bob is a record dude. A record dude is a man—sorry, no dudettes—that lives, eats, and breathes vinyl. They can tell you what label Matthew Sweet is on, tell you who produced the third Santana album, and what row they sat in for Mick's birthday party in 1971 at MSG. With the advent of CDs and mp3s, the art of the liner note has gone the way of Yiddish. Almost extinct! There just isn't room to write about the album on such small or nonexistent packaging. This has reduced the number of record dudes as well, but they still exist. And I still love to chat with them. After all, while not a *true* record dude, I'm pretty decent.

Bob lived in central New Jersey and was now a band manager. In 1999, Bob decided to throw a birthday party for his 40th. Since his turf was the Jersey Shore, he enlisted many of his musician friends to play at his party. It was soon after that Bob was diagnosed with Parkinson's disease. In light of the success of his party, he decided to have another party, but this time, it would be a fundraiser for Parkinson's. He has done it every year since and has raised over $1 million.

We decided to meet for dinner the following night. It was there that we learned we had a mutual friend in Mark Michel and that we lived in neighboring NJ towns. We check in with one another from time to time, and I consider him a friend and fundraising role model.

Harry Chapin

Summer of '72

The radio included a very heavy rotation of Donna Fargo—I love the biopic the Coen brothers made about her life—Edward (Teddy) Bear, and Harry Chapin. Of the three, Harry left an impression.

The following summer, I went to an overnight camp in Bucks County Pennsylvania called Camp Nock-A-Mixon. I am still friendly with many of the people I met that summer. I was turning 16 in August, so I was sure to bring my own music with me. David Bowie, Humble Pie, Pink Floyd, and Jethro Tull were all packed in my trunk. I thought my roster of musicians would help me make some friends. I was wrong about that. Instead, I was met by Jim Croce, Elton John, Neil diamond, Jimmy Buffett, and other light rock stalwarts. My one musical kindred spirit was Scott Hammer. He had Aerosmith, Frank Zappa, and unbelievably, Harry Chapin. We developed a friendship that is still going strong some 41 years later. He and I have seen Harry perform at the State Theatre in New Brunswick, My Father's Place in Roslyn, NY, and at The Bottom Line in Manhattan.

Harry Chapin basically invented the rock musician call for charity. His relationship with Oxfam—the world hunger organization—helped set the stage for The Concert for Bangladesh and Live Aid, among many others. It was during the fall of 1976 when our paths crossed. He was scheduled to appear at Trinity Church, a small church right outside the gates of Georgetown University. I was all over that. I was one of the first people in line, and I got a seat in the center of the second row.

He came without his band and had entertained the (almost) full church for what seemed like a few hours when it finally came time to sing Taxi, his first radio hit. He said, *"Usually when I sing Taxi, Big John Wallace sings the high-pitched interlude, but he's not here today. Does anybody want to come up on stage and sing with me?"* It was almost a reflexive motion; my arm went up, and he pointed at it. The next thing I knew, *I was Big John Wallace!*

It's supposed to be sung in a high-pitched tone, which I did not do, but I evidently gave someone in the back some material. He yelled at me across the theater: *"Hey! Cross your legs!"*

Harry died in a car crash a few years later. His legacy is rich in charity, and in my memory.

Piano Lessons

Piano Lesson! Practice! *"Good King Wenceslas," "Blue Danube"*
Piano lesson. Practice. *"Punchball," "Ringolevyo," "Johnny on the Pony"*
Piano . . . lessen . . .

Kickball!!

This was the evolution—the wasting of my musical talent.

As an 8 year old, I was quite good. My lessons with Mrs. Emerling were smooth, but my mind was elsewhere. I was good enough to be invited to begin a recital by playing "The Star-Spangled Banner." Also on the docket were Cousins Leo and Sherry, probably playing something equally patriotic. I guess I peaked early; this exhibition of Americana was the highlight of my piano-playing career. I can still play the melody to the tune with one hand.

At the time, no way did I want to practice. I wanted to play baseball! My ball playing diversion, which began with coach Bernie Koretz and O'Rourke Excavation when I was in the fourth grade, went all the way up to high school senior. I know the cliché says never give up on your dreams, but I think that phone call from the New York Mets did not get lost in my voicemail, nor do I believe there could be a message in my spam folder.

Satchel Paige pitched when he was in his sixties. I want to take the mound for the Mets for 2 reasons: (1) to try to strike someone out, and (2) so I can "shake off" a catcher's sign.

I can dream, can't I? Not this one!

Saturday in the Park with Mike

Every July, a fund raising softball game is held in Central Park promoted by Mike Costa. Mike is a Long Island accountant who, thankfully, has fundraising skills that far surpass his softball skills. He has raised millions of dollars for PD. When I heard about it, I had to participate.

My post high school softball career started strong with two intramural championships as a member of George's International Fruit Market at Georgetown. I played in a variety of leagues until I was about 30. It was at this point that I noticed that my game had eluded me. It got to the point where if I tried to play third base, a suit of armor would be necessary when once a protective cup would be enough. At bat, I could still swing and make contact, but the outfielders could play an entire game of Yahtzee when I got up. My line drive ability was gone.

I spoke to Mike, and he was as nice as could be, inviting me to come by and participate however I wanted. I wanted to hit homeruns and be on the cover of *Sports Illustrated*, but I'd take 1 inning and 1 at bat. I did get to play the whole game, and did get a hit, but that wasn't the highlight. The people I met included celebrities who were eager to engage me in conversation as I was the only PD patient involved who was actually there to play.

The actor, Tony Lo Bianco, invited me to see him in *Fiorello!* Tito Landrum told me about each of his World Series rings, and Babe Ruth's daughter was the nicest woman, telling me all about the Babe. However, the best story involves a lesser celebrity. On the show *Everybody Loves Raymond*, the brother, Robert, has a dog named Shamsky. Art Shamsky was a journeyman baseball player with a 253 lifetime average and 68 home runs. Cooperstown doesn't know his phone number, but because of his Jewishness, he is still—even today—a New York hero.

I can't speak for other ethnic groups, but Jews and professional sports is such a rare combination that whenever lightning strikes, we exalt the occasion.

Ron Bloomberg was the American League's first designated hitter. Hank Greenberg was a certified slugger. The early years of the NBA had Dolph Schayes. But the Jewish mother of all such marriages was that of New York and Sandy Koufax. Not only was he Jewish, he was from Brooklyn. His refusal to pitch the opening game of the World Series on Yom Kippur is as monumental in Jewish folklore as any story from the *Torah*, the *Talmud*, or *The Modern Jewish Cookbook*. Neither Albert Einstein, Sigmund Freud, nor Anne Frank herself was as beloved. He still goes to spring training, offers pitching advice, and is notoriously elusive to the press. Every Jew of that era remembers that World Series event as if it was V-J Day.

You can imagine the excitement when I was at the registration table and overheard the tall man before me say, *"Hello, I'm Art Shamsky."* I once made the mistake of not approaching a celebrity when I had something appropriate to say. I wasn't going to blow this one.

After I registered, I found him and said the following (more or less):
> *Hi, my name is Alan Jackowitz, and I want you to know that in the summer of '68 or '69, I was at a game the same night you came off the disabled list. It was late in the game, and the situation called for a lefty pinch hitter. The crowd erupted into 'WE WANT SHAMSKY!' 'WE WANT SHAMSKY!' Sure enough, there you were in the on deck circle, donut on bat, loosening up. The crowd erupted! You got up to the plate and lined a single into left center—pandemonium!*

Without a moment's hesitation, Shamsky said to me—I can call him Shamsky because we are friends—

"Cecil Upshaw threw that pitch, a fastball down and away."

My trip to New York was made without even one pitch being thrown. For me, he became a hero again, 40 years later.

"People Who Died"

Jim Carroll was an urban poet who rose to fame in the '70s with his book *The Basketball Diaries* and the song "People Who Died." I did not read the book, but I loved the song. The song has a great, fast rhythm to it, but I'm not sure why I like the song so much. It might be because the lyrics have an ordinariness to them that belies the gravity of the people's deaths. Similar to the scene in *Taxi Driver* when De Niro kills Keitel almost matter-of-factly, Carroll rattles off names and their causes of death like it was a substitute teacher calling roll. *"They were all my friends, and they died."*

Below is a list of a few people whose deaths have influenced me in a profound way. The fact that I'm recalling them now highlights this fact. No death is matter-of-fact. My remembrance of the lives below illustrates that fact.

There are 4 reasons why I've decided to include the people below:
- to pay homage to these friends or acquaintances whose life still lies within me, subliminally
- to question what the world lost from the premature demise of these potential heroes next door—a premature death robs us of what they would have accomplished
- to show their families that their memory Is still alive
- Parkinson's, while being an awful disease, still pales in comparison to what is possible

Girl on East 5th Street in my first grade class—Having heard gunshots, my father came flying into my room to protect me. Not necessary, father daughter murder suicide. Illustrating Mental illness, frailty of life, my father's protective impulses.

Steve Goldwasser—murdered in California while hitchhiking, came to my Bar Mitzvah. Impossible to tackle in football.

Jim Rishar—high school math teacher, said everyone knows when they are going to be sick as the day before progresses. Please let me know, I'll do the same. He didn't. His death affected me profoundly—if he was wearing a seat belt, he would have been unscathed.

Mrs. Hoffman's father—Nixon's inauguration, January 20, 1969. Came back from lunch. Girl brought a note that left our teacher sobbing.

Sandy Roberts—by now, he might have earned an Academy Award. His future was unlimited. He died in a car crash while at USC film school, age 19. He was a great friend of Eric's. Not even his unimaginable death could stop him from smiling down on us.

"you're gonna have to serve somebody"

Bob Dylan wrote: "It may be the devil or it may be the Lord / But you're gonna have to serve somebody."

I think that a Dylan themed restaurant would be fantastic. A rosy cheeked 19-year-old college girl would come to your table, write her name upside down on your tablecloth, probably "Amber" or something, and say, *"Welcome to Zimmy's! Can I start you off with an appeteaser? Our nachos are positively forthright."* With such a catalog of songs, think of all the Dylanesque food possibilities:

- *Maggie's Farm* fresh eggs
- *One More Cup of Coffee*
- *Tangled Up in Blue* plate special
- *Girl from the North Country* fried steak

Of course when you call the restaurant, a gruff voice would answer, *"It's a pensive, introspective, thoughtful, wonderful, loving, prolific, cloudy, sunny, rainy, snowy, hot, humid, day at Zimmy's. Can I help you . . . ?"* (unintelligibly!)

October 2011: Dylan is coming to Nova Southeastern University to do a concert. I didn't buy any tickets in advance. I was always a reasonable Dylan fan, enjoyed some songs, but not the performances. It is now 4 o'clock on the day of the show, and I'm in the school's cafeteria. There's a life-size cutout of Dylan by the cashier. I casually ask the cashier if she is excited about Bob Dylan playing at the gym this evening. You have to admire her honesty. She has no clue who Bob Dylan is. There is no mirror behind the register, but I'm sure the look on my face, which usually bears a Parkinson's imprint, looks like that of a bystander to a house fire. There are 4 people behind me in line, so I do my best George Gallup and ask them if they know who Bob Dylan is. 0 for 5. Now, I am on fire!

You don't have to like Bob Dylan; you don't even have to know any more than "Blowing in the Wind," "Like a Rolling Stone," "Positively 4th Street," or "Mr. Tambourine Man," but you do have to know who he is, his contribution to American culture, or just the fact that he is the father of that guy from the Wallflowers. Bob Dylan should be an answer to a question on the naturalization processing application. I'm still steaming from that day in the cafeteria!

On the way out of the show, my brother Robert and I were accosted by 2 college kids. Their pick up line failed miserably, *"Hey, you guys look like you've been to prior Dylan shows."* This was obviously code for *"You guys are older than fuck."* They wanted to pick our brains about how this show compared to others, and generally about music since the seventies They didn't know that they hit the mother lode. They also resurrected my day. We went to the school café, and for two hours, I did my best Studs Terkel, providing them with an oral history of concert going in America from Sly and the Family Stone at Madison Square Gardens—Dec. 1971, through Spoon—Revolution 2013. What began with the death knell of the end of our civilization, ended with the hope that our few remaining curious citizens will lead the way.

The show itself was a revelation: about midway through I realized that my stiffness was gone. The vaunted Bob Dylan dance music was so infectious that I boogied away some symptoms. I now know first hand that there is medical proof of the therapeutic value of music. That's a copayment I'm happy to pay.

Today

Yesterday was the 7th anniversary of my Parkinson's Diagnosis.
Today is my 57th birthday.
My mind is swimming with a world of thoughts.

At this stage of our lives, everybody's got something. My friends—virtual and across the table—have encountered a surfeit of woes: divorce, bankruptcy, death of a child, death of a spouse, death, unemployment. No one is immune. It's called *life*. It has been said that if we all sat around a table and threw our issues into the middle, and had the ability to pick up anybody's, we'd pick ours up, again. I could do without the drool, however.

After the death of Robin Williams, much was written of his depression and lifelong struggles with addiction. I couldn't begin to chronicle his career any better than what's been done. What I fear is that the general uninformed public is going to draw the wrong conclusion in light of the statement his wife made regarding his Parkinson's diagnosis. What killed him was his depression. PD was one more straw on the camel's back of issues that Robin faced. Someone with a PD diagnosis should look to Michael J. Fox, Brian Grant, Muhammad Ali, Janet Reno, and countless others who've lived productive lives despite the diagnosis. Perhaps they should come out publicly and make such statements. We lost what could have been the BEST spokesperson for bringing money and awareness to the cause to find a cure. Furthermore, depression is still a taboo subject that affects people of all ages. College-aged suicide is way too rampant. If you break your leg, you go to an orthopedist. If you're clinically depressed, you see the appropriate medical professional—no taboo. See the doc; get treated.

Vbar

On 225 Sullivan Street, there lives an establishment that provides a haven for anybody traipsing through The Village. For me, it was Cheers, Central Perk, and your neighborhood bar and coffee shop all wrapped into The Drunken Clam. It was all of that and more.

My love affair started the summer I took Hayley for orientation at NYU. I dropped her off and had about 3 hours to kill. Walking down Sullivan Street—no, I didn't run into Mr. Cacciatore or Adam Duritz—I found Matt Denny at V Bar. Red hair, 35-40, humble coolness emanating as he asked for my drink order. What also immediately struck me, was the music in the background—"Mess Around" by Ray Charles"—quickly becoming the foreground. I spent the entire 3 hours trading music stories, song recommendations, even NY Jet and Yankee stories with Matt as this lazy, hot summer afternoon evolved from what could have been an aimless stroll through lower Manhattan to the beginning of friendships and a beacon broadcasting from Greenwich Village.

My days in NY were filled with work. My nights often ended at V Bar. It has been the only time I've ever been a regular at a bar, and if I had a bucket list, that would've been on it. The initial reason was the quality of the bartenders and the music they played. In addition to Matt, Kevin Condon and Chris Kmet easily formed the triumvirate of NY bartenders. Kevin is a 30ish writer and photographer from NC who will engage you on any topic with very strong opinions. His musical tastes run from Nick Cave and Tom Waits to Elvis Costello and any older band I might recommend. If you ask him to play a song, you'll hear it . . . the next night you are there. Maybe. You have to earn clout via discussion. But it will be a rich one.

Chris is 35-40 with a look and spirit resembling Denis Leary. From Chicago, he embodies a workingman's sensibility while having fun tending bar. He's the guy with the bar jokes, some of which I still get mileage out of. For example: *Three turtles were drinking at a bar late one night. At midnight, the bartender cut them off. "Get the hell out of here you drunk turtles!" They scamper on home. While on their way, one has to pee. He veers off into the woods and begins to pee. While there, he gets accosted by a gang of angry snails. They beat the crap out of him. They break his shell and leave him one inch from death. The next morning, a cop sees him and asks, "Oh, my God! What happened to you?" The turtle says, "I have no idea. Everything happened so fast."*

The cast of characters that are called "regulars" is impressively long and deep. In order of regularity:

Paul: 55ish marketer, aura of intelligence with depth of feeling that makes him easily likeable. He looks professorial, but his love of Jobim, Sinatra, and Daft Punk shows an eclecticism that is anything but.

Ricky: 27ish filmmaker, self-deprecating humor about his black gayness in a seemingly white straight establishment. Self confident, a fixture at the bar as he lives above it.

Tracy: 70ish woman with an Irish/British accent. Soft spoken. Almost a ward of NYU housing, she parks her walker in the bar's cellar each night. Whoever is on duty does the fetching. She sings "Danny Boy" for the bar on St. Patty's Day. When I came by after she had already sung, she gave me a special encore.

Nate: 30ish raucous, fun loving, complex filmmaker. Became his buddy while explaining my PD to him. I told him about my experience on the bus. Short steps give me trouble, thus buses give me trouble. As I slithered out that day, I heard a voice from the street below call out, *"HURRY UP!"* As I progressed further, I saw that the shrill voice belonged to an old woman with a walker. I howled as I asked her how many miles per gallon she got. Nate howled as I told him the story.

Jim Hughes: 65 year old doctor who at best was fodder for ridicule and at worst was a Nazi. He couldn't complete one sentence without telling you which degrees from Oxford, Cambridge, Harvard, Fordham, and Stanley Kaplan had been bestowed on him. One day, he said he had 98 albums by an obscure reggae artist. I asked him how many existed in total. He responded *"105."* I said, *"What the hell are you doing here wasting time? Go get the other 7!"* Matt said it was the funniest thing he had ever heard in a bar. I love that.

Francesca, Krystle, the girl who shares my birthday from England.

And so on…

The common thread among all these people is the community they have created. The big city can be lonely, and here was a clubhouse to make it less so. In my case, it created the first platform for me to tell my PD story. People at the bar were amazed at my humor and resilience in dealing with the disease. I was Norm at the end of the bar, though less drunk, and more wise. This was a place where everybody knew my name for the right reasons.

"Why me?"

This is a question I haven't asked myself, but let's play with it for a while.

First, whom would I be asking? The picture painted when asked aloud is that of a George Bailey type with arms and gaze pointing to the sky and a nondenominational God. I'm not a very religious person, if "religious" means going to temple or church or mosque and following the service rituals. I was born into a Jewish home. We were conservative because that was the temple closest to our house. Reconstructionist is the wing of the religion that holds the dogma closest to my beliefs. There isn't a big throne in the sky holding a man with a long white beard who is looking down and pulling strings that move us all like marionettes. Rabbi Andrew Jacobs of Ramat Shalom Synagogue explained the Reconstructionist movement to me. He said, "God exists in all of us through the good deeds we do." By the same token, the pulpit is not a raised platform, but the same height, so as not to show superiority.

So following this rationale, God has bestowed upon me this disease with the supposition that I will be able to turn this huge negative into something quite positive. The ability to empathize with the disease stricken and take the fuel that is given me through music, humor, and every day personal interactions and turn it into at least one smile is truly a gift that I cherish.

The scientific answer to *"Why me?"* is appealing to the logical accountant part of me. My mother has it; my genetic profile shows a high chance of getting it. I'm a member of the Ashkenazi Jews, a group with an elevated risk of getting it.

Everybody gets something. My something is PD. If I've been cursed with this disease, I've also been blessed with the resiliency to press on undeterred, and for that, I'm grateful.

The cause of the disease doesn't matter. Whether it's divine intervention, genetics, or environment, if I have the ability to ease suffering by telling a joke, or playing a song, or just waking most days with a smile, that's a gift I'm proud to have and must put to use. Though it took 50 years to know that I have it, there is no expiration date.

Now that we've played, let's see the facts:
The pleasure I get from somebody telling me I'm inspirational is fabulous.
The pleasure that I get from my two fantastic children cuts to my soul.
Maybe, just maybe, it is no coincidence that both of them are world-class musicians.

God certainly works in mysterious ways.

Acknowledgments

Judie, Eric, Hayley, Arthur, Ina, Robert, Lori, Richard, Lonny Schwartz, Larry Friedman, Gary Kleinman, Sue Cimbricz, Brendan Flynn, Shauna Sweeney, @KingsHeadPub, The Manor staff, Matt Denny, Chris Kmet, Kevin Condon, Jayne Bonilla, Betsy Berg, Mitchell Radist, Glenn Grekin, Steven Silverman, Jay Spitz, Scott Schecter, Scott Hammer, Phil McNally, Joe Razzano, Rick Harris, Mike Baker, Richard Micek, Dr. Carey, Dr. Carlos Singer, Dr. Barry Cutler, Gary Segal, Barry Blattman, Shonti Bruce, Chris McDonough,

Judie, Eric, Hayley, Daltrey

My family! My motivation!! None of this would be possible without them.
Let's meet them in reverse order:

> Daltrey – recently deceased Bichon Frise that we gave an extra 15 years of life, named for his long curls, as opposed to his '70s era fringed vest. Our neighbor, Toni, worked in a building that housed an agency dedicated to placing pets with the elderly. When one woman became too infirm to care for her dog, her daughter tried to return him to the agency. When the agency said *"no,"* Toni took him home and offered him to us. I never had a dog before, so when my kids said that I had no responsibility for walking him, I took them at their word. Now, I know their word is meaningless. I don't trust them with anything whatsoever. If they said it was sunny outside, I'd grab my umbrella and look for myself. Not only did *I* walk him, *they* never did.
>
> Hayley—nicknames include Tessie, Tessie Cat, *Tess of the d'Urbervilles*, Tweety. She was originally nicknamed Tweety because of her slow to come in hair. Now, her singing might get her the same nickname. Most families have ups and downs, Hayley's ratio of ups to downs is skewed low due to her birthdate. It is said that what doesn't go your way makes you stronger; Hayley's strength coach would be impressed. When Hayley puts her mind to getting something done, laser beam focus is invoked, and it gets done.   Learning to ride a bike, shooting a layup, getting into NYU—all required this focus, and she still uses it. I admire this perseverance as a remarkable achievement.
>   Eric was taking piano lessons, because Judie and I

thought it would be a good idea before learning drums. After a few weeks, his teacher stopped and told us he should go straight to drum lessons. The teacher pointed to Hayley and said, *"Get up on the bench, and finish the lesson."* Results? Nine straight superior ratings in the countywide assessments. With the help of her singing teacher, Cheryl Long, she flourished as a singer. When it came time to apply to college, the only school she wanted to attend was NYU. NYU wanted her more. Her career has NO limits.

Eric— primary nickname: Schnoppy. He was born drumming and has almost unbelievably stayed consistently on a trajectory to greatness. His career is as steady as the pocket he creates while drumming. Despite his dedication to and his success from his craft, what he really wants to do is (don't worry not direct) . . . comedy! His collaboration with his friend Sandy, who unbelievably was killed in an auto accident, is legendary here in FL. They performed as standups at open mic night at the Fort Lauderdale Improv. He once thanked me for exposing him to *Monty Python* at an early age.

    My respect for Eric transcends music. He was born— and remained—overweight through his childhood. As a college sophomore, Eric lost a lot of the weight and has kept it off ever since: a remarkable achievement.

Judie—nicknames include Pinky (from *Adam's Rib*), younger than me, World's Best Mother, My Best Friend. An inner strength—despite an upbringing shrouded in adoption, divorce, and moving at 16—enables all of our success.

About the Author

Alan Jackowitz...you are now up to speed!

www.ingramcontent.com/pod-product-compliance
Lightning Source LLC
Chambersburg PA
CBHW061250040426
42444CB00010B/2340